The Underground Railroad

The Underground Railroad

Dennis Brindell Fradin

 **Marshall Cavendish** Benchmark

New York

Dedication

For my wife and co-everything, Judy, with Love

Marshall Cavendish Benchmark
99 White Plains Road
Tarrytown, New York 10591-5502
www.marshallcavendish.us

Text and maps copyright © 2009 by Marshall Cavendish Corporation
Maps by Rodica Prato

All Internet sites were available and accurate when sent to press.

Library of Congress Cataloging-in-Publication Data
Fradin, Dennis B.
The Underground Railroad / by Dennis Brindell Fradin.
p. cm. — (Turning points in U.S. history)
Summary: "Covers the development of the Underground Railroad as a
watershed event in U.S. history, influencing social, economic, and political
policies that shaped the nation's future"—Provided by publisher.
Includes bibliographical references and index.
ISBN 978-0-7614-3014-8
1. Underground railroad—Juvenile literature. 2. Antislavery
movements—United States—History—19th century—Juvenile literature.
3. Fugitive slaves—United States—History—19th century—Juvenile literature.
I. Title.
E450.F775 2008
973.7'115—dc22
2007030448

Photo research by Connie Gardner

Cover: This 1867 painting by Theodor Kaufmann depicts a group of slaves moving "On to Liberty."
Title page: Eastman Johnson's *ca.*1862 painting captures "The Ride for Liberty, The Fugitive Slaves."
Cover photo by The Art Archive/Metropolitan Museum of Art, New York/Laurie Platt Winfrey
The photographs in this book are used by permission and through the courtesy of: *Granger Collection:* 3, 29, 32; *Getty Images:* Hulton Archive, 6, 36;
Bridgeman Art Library: Field Workers on the Hopkinton plantation, South Carolina, 1862 (photo) by American Photographer, © Private Collection/Peter
Newark American Pictures, 10; John Hancock (1737-93) signs the American Declaration of Independence, 4th July 1776 (colour litho) by American School,
© Private Collection/Peter Newark American Pictures, 14; The Underground Railroad Aids with a Runaway Slave by Arthur Bowen Davies (1862-1928),
© Private Collection, 26, 40-41; *The Image Works:* Topham, 12; Corbis: 17; Layne Kennedy, 18; Louis Psihoyos, 23; *NorthWind Picture Archives:* 21, 28, 30, 35;
Art Resource: Schomburg Center, 30.

Editor: Deborah Grahame
Publisher: Michelle Bisson
Art Director: Anahid Hamparian

Printed in Malaysia
1 3 5 6 4 2

Contents

CHAPTER ONE: Slavery in the Thirteen Colonies   7

CHAPTER TWO: To Be a Slave   11

CHAPTER THREE: "Life, Liberty, and the Pursuit of Happiness"   15

CHAPTER FOUR: The Rise of the Underground Railroad   19

CHAPTER FIVE: The Underground Railroad in Action   27

CHAPTER SIX: The South Strikes Back   33

                  Glossary   38

                  Timeline   40

                  Further Information   43

                  Bibliography   45

                  Index   47

English men are shown guarding a group of people they intend to bring as slaves to the New World.

CHAPTER ONE

Slavery in the Thirteen Colonies

England settled Virginia, its first American colony, in 1607. Twelve years later, in 1619, about twenty African people arrived by ship at Jamestown, Virginia. They were among the first black slaves brought into England's American colonies.

After establishing Virginia, England founded or took over twelve more American colonies. Thousands of African slaves were shipped in to do work for the colonists. Some colonists **protested** that **slavery** was wrong. In 1688 people in Germantown (now part of Philadelphia), Pennsylvania, issued an **antislavery declaration**. It was the first **resolution** condemning slavery in what is now the United States.

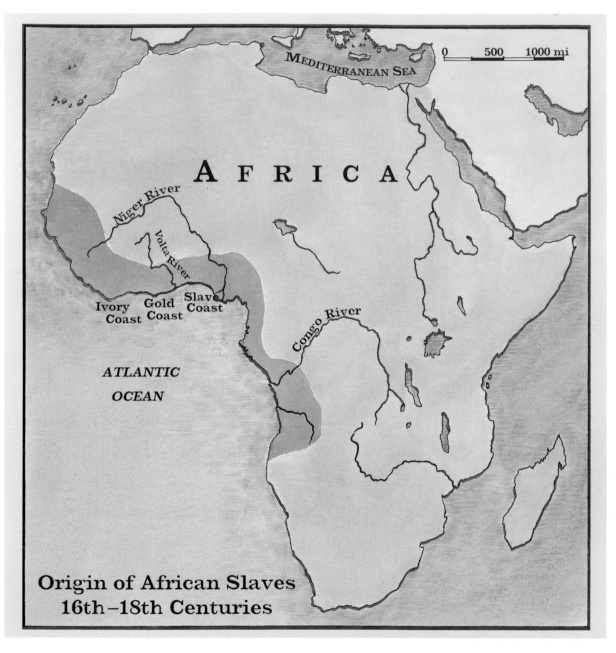

0   500   1000 mi

MEDITERRANEAN SEA

AFRICA

Niger River

Volta River

Ivory
Coast

Gold
Coast

Slave
Coast

Congo River

ATLANTIC

OCEAN

**Origin of African Slaves
16th–18th Centuries**

Most slaves came from West Africa, the regions shown here as shaded areas. People were packed in slave ships by the hundreds, and many died before reaching the colonies.

Still, all thirteen colonies allowed slavery. In the 1770s the colonial slave **population** reached half a million. Not counting American Indians, one-fifth of the people in the thirteen colonies were black slaves.

Field hands on a large South Carolina farm pose for a photograph in 1862.

CHAPTER TWO

To Be a Slave

To be a slave meant that another person owned you. By law, slaves had to do what their owners ordered. Disobedient slaves might be whipped or even put to death.

Most slaves, including children as young as seven years old, were field hands. They grew tobacco, rice, cotton, and other crops for their owners. Field hands and their families lived in log huts. They were fed corn and bacon that was often moldy. They worked from sunup to sundown. If they fell behind in their work, their owners whipped them.

Other African Americans were house slaves. They cooked, cleaned, and took care of their owners' children. House slaves generally had a

The photograph is sweet, but the disturbing fact is that this child's caregiver was owned by her family as property.

better life than field hands. In many cases they wore their owners' old clothing, ate their leftovers, and lived in their homes.

All slaves were bound by certain rules. To start with, they were considered property. They had no more rights than a dog or a horse. Most slaves did not even have last names of their own. Instead, they were given their owners' last name. Slaves were not allowed to learn to read and write. Owners were afraid that educated slaves might gather together and plan a revolt.

Slaves' families tended to be very close, for the only thing they had was each other. This meant little to their owners. Many masters sold their slaves to make money. This broke families apart.

Naturally, slaves wanted to escape these harsh conditions and to be free. From the early days of slavery in the American colonies, slaves tried to escape. Many of them were captured. As punishment, they were branded like cattle, sold far from home, or killed.

Not all African Americans were slaves. In the early and mid-1800s, one-eighth of the African Americans in the American colonies were free blacks. Sometimes owners set their slaves free by writing it in their wills. Other free blacks were the children or grandchildren of people who had escaped slavery.

Some slaves were able to buy their **liberty** from their owners. On most **plantations**, slaves had Sundays off. Slaves who worked on Sundays were paid small wages. By saving their money over many years, some slaves earned enough to buy their freedom.

John Hancock is shown signing the Declaration of Independence.

CHAPTER THREE

"Life, Liberty, and the Pursuit of Happiness"

On July 4, 1776, American leaders issued the Declaration of Independence. This document explained that the thirteen colonies were breaking free from Britain. They were now a new nation—the United States of America.

The Declaration of Independence stated that everyone was entitled to "Life, liberty, and the pursuit of happiness." Some Americans asked: Might the slaves deserve their liberty, too? Should the declaration do something to free them? All thirteen states still permitted slavery, however. Slave owners depended on African Americans to run their plantations. As a result, American leaders decided that the Declaration would not condemn slavery.

A Virginia plantation owner and his family tour the slaves' quarters during the 1700s.

The young country's leaders created the nation's Constitution, or framework of government, in 1787. Some Northern states had ended slavery by then. In the South, though, slavery was bigger than ever. By the 1780s, the South was home to about 90 percent of the country's 600,000 slaves.

Several framers of the Constitution wanted it to outlaw slavery. However, some Southern leaders would not sign a Constitution that did this. To keep the peace, the opponents of slavery backed down. Like the Declaration of Independence, the Constitution did not take a stand against slavery.

An illustration titled "Effects of the Fugitive Slave Law" depicts slaves being shot at as they try to escape their owners.

Slaveholders won another victory six years later. Owners were angry about losing slaves who fled to Northern states where slavery was **illegal**. In response, the U.S. Congress passed the **Fugitive** Slave Law of 1793. Helping a slave escape became a **federal** crime. The new law also allowed slaveholders to cross state lines and to reclaim their runaway slaves by showing ownership papers to public officials.

This safe house near the Ohio River was owned by an organizer of the Underground Railroad.

CHAPTER FOUR

The Rise of the Underground Railroad

Many Americans believed in a "higher law" than U.S. laws that protected slavery. This was the law of right and wrong. These Americans began to disobey federal law by helping large numbers of slaves escape. In the early 1800s they established a network of people and hiding places that became known as the Underground Railroad.

Fugitive slaves often followed certain routes. For example, many slaves from Delaware and Maryland fled to freedom in eastern Pennsylvania. Slaves from Kentucky often traveled through Indiana before settling in Ohio and other northern areas. Antislavery families along these routes allowed fugitive slaves to stop in their homes for food and rest.

A Matter of Faith

Many people became part of the Underground Railroad because their religious beliefs taught that slavery was wrong. The Quakers, also called the Religious Society of Friends, were extremely active in the Underground Railroad. Congregationalists, Presbyterians, Methodists, Baptists, Jewish people, and people of other faiths also helped slaves escape.

Slaves who escaped Southern plantations usually fled at night. Some fugitives fled alone, but many others escaped in groups. The fugitives often traveled on foot and covered about fifteen miles per night. On clear nights, they made sure they were heading northward by following the North Star. If it was cloudy, they used the moss that grew on the north side of trees to point them in the right direction.

Runaways were in the greatest danger while still in the South. There, few people were willing or able to shelter them. Until they reached the North, runaways hid in caves, woods, and swamps during the day. At night they continued their northward journey.

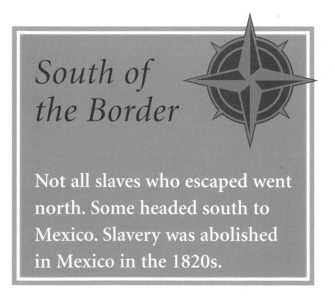

South of the Border

Not all slaves who escaped went north. Some headed south to Mexico. Slavery was abolished in Mexico in the 1820s.

Wading through swamps was among the unpleasant ordeals that slaves endured in their journey to freedom in the North.

The Underground Railroad helped slaves mainly after they reached a Northern state. How did runaways recognize safe houses along the way? Perhaps back on the plantation they had heard of an **abolitionist** family living in a certain place. Some Underground Railroad families put a lantern in their yard as a signal that fugitive slaves were welcome in their home.

Near dawn the fugitives would try to find an Underground Railroad house. They used a special knock to gain entry to some houses. The family in the house would provide the fugitives with a place to sleep by day.

Money Hunters

Many owners offered large rewards for their runaway slaves. The reward for catching a slave might be one hundred dollars, two hundred dollars, or even five hundred dollars. Slave hunters knew they would make a lot of money if they tracked slaves into Northern states. This was a big reason why Northerners tried to keep their Underground Railroad work secret, even though their region did not allow slavery.

They would feed the runaways and give them fresh clothes. Before nightfall their hosts would tell the slaves where the next safe house was located—ten or fifteen miles farther along. After dark the fugitives would set out northward once again.

Owners sometimes tracked their slaves to an Underground Railroad house. The fugitives would hide in closets and secret rooms. Slave hunters complained that runaway slaves seemed to disappear in certain places as if they had boarded an underground train. This is how the network of people and hiding places became known as the Underground Railroad.

The Underground Railroad helped escapees until they reached a city thought to be beyond their owners' reach. Two such places were

Detroit, Michigan, and Boston, Massachusetts. Other cities included Chicago, Illinois; Oberlin, Ohio; Philadelphia, Pennsylvania; Rochester, New York; and various towns in Canada. Runaways changed their names so that their former owners would have a hard time finding them. They settled down in their new homes to live as free people.

Since helping slaves escape was illegal, the people of the Underground Railroad devised a secret language. They used railroad terms. Houses where slaves were sheltered became known as stations or depots. People who sheltered escaped slaves were stationmasters. Men and women who helped guide fugitives northward were conductors. The fugitives were called cargo, goods, or passengers. People who

A Gettysburg, Pennsylvania homeowner created a sliding shelf to conceal a crawl space where several slaves could hide.

23

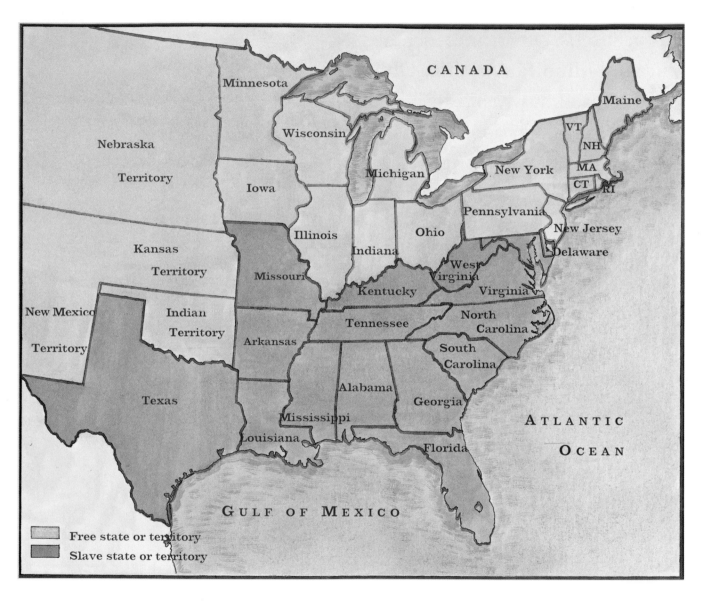

This map shows slave and free states and territories in 1860.

A Railroad off the Map

The activities of the Underground Railroad were illegal, so it was organized loosely. It had no mailing address. There was no list of its members. No single person oversaw its activities. Much of its work happened by word of mouth. For example, after church someone might mention that a thirty-mile stretch of land in Ohio or Indiana had no Underground Railroad station. An abolitionist family might decide to move to that area in order to help fugitive slaves.

helped fugitives establish a new life on free soil were brakemen. The Underground Railroad itself was sometimes referred to as the UGRR.

People on the UGRR used their code to protect runaway slaves. They could discuss their work without worrying that someone would hear them. They could always claim they were just talking about trains.

A painting depicts Underground Railroad workers helping an escaped slave avoid discovery by slave hunters.

CHAPTER FIVE

The Underground Railroad in Action

Between the early 1800s and 1860, about 100,000 Southern slaves escaped to free soil. Thousands of UGRR workers helped them. Details about most of the escapes remain unknown. What we do know comes from books written by escaped slaves and UGRR workers.

Levi and Catherine Coffin were prominent stationmasters on the Underground Railroad. Between 1826 and 1847, they sheltered more than two thousand slaves at their home in Newport (now Fountain City), Indiana. Slave hunters from Kentucky once tracked a group of runaways to Levi and Catherine's home. Meanwhile, the couple hid the slaves in secret rooms. The slave hunters were frustrated that the fugitives had vanished.

Levi Coffin (1798–1877) was born and raised in North Carolina, a slave state, but as a Quaker he was opposed to slavery.

One of them said, "There must be an underground railroad, and Levi Coffin must be its president." This is one version of how the name *Underground Railroad* was coined.

In 1847 Levi and Catherine moved to Cincinnati, Ohio. There they sheltered 1,100 fugitive slaves. This raised the total number of slaves they helped to more than 3,100.

A Maryland slave named Harriet Tubman made her dash for liberty in 1849. She followed the North Star toward Pennsylvania. A farmer helped Tubman by hiding her in his wagon and driving her part of the way. She later told a friend that once she reached free soil,

I looked at my hands to see if I was the same person. There was such a glory over everything. The Sun came like gold through the trees, and over the fields, and I felt like I was in Heaven.

Gaining her own freedom was not enough for Tubman. She decided to rescue other slaves from **bondage**. Tubman learned the locations of numerous UGRR stations. Over the next ten years, she made roughly thirteen trips into the South. She helped about 150 slaves escape and led most of them to freedom herself. If babies without parents came along, she carried them in baskets on her arms.

Tubman became the Underground Railroad's most famous conductor. Maryland slaveholders offered $12,000 for her capture, but she was never caught. She stayed away from slave hunters by disguising herself, sometimes as an old woman.

Harriet Tubman (ca. 1820–1913) became known as the "Moses of her people."

A favorite station of Tubman's was the home of Thomas Garrett in Wilmington, Delaware. This stationmaster aided about 2,500 escaped slaves. One time when police officers were looking for Tubman and some of her "passengers" along the Wilmington bridge, she and Garrett made a plan. In the morning, they sent two wagonloads of bricklayers across the bridge as though they were going to work. The guards let them pass and assumed they would cross the bridge again that evening. The bricklayers did cross the bridge again. This time, though, Tubman and her "passengers" were hiding in the wagons under the bricks.

A photograph of William Still, taken years after his UGRR efforts

Tubman's African-American friend William Still was a leading UGRR brakeman. Still ran the Pennsylvania Anti-Slavery Society office. He helped hundreds of escaped slaves who arrived on the free soil of Philadelphia.

Still was involved in an unusual escape in March 1849. Samuel A. Smith, an UGRR worker in Richmond, Virginia, sent Still a telegram. It said that a "case of goods" would soon arrive in Philadelphia. Smith packed a slave named Henry Brown into a box that supposedly held a shipment of shoes. For about thirty hours Brown was squished inside the crate as he traveled by train and steamboat to Philadelphia. He breathed through three little holes. He had biscuits to eat and a container of water to drink. Finally, the box arrived at the Anti-Slavery Society

A Long Tale of Escape

In 1848 Ellen and William Craft made a daring escape from slavery. Ellen was a light-skinned African American. Her husband was dark. Ellen dressed in men's clothing and pretended to be a white man named Mr. Johnson. William pretended to be Mr. Johnson's slave. The couple then traveled on trains and steamboats one thousand miles from Georgia, to free soil in Pennsylvania. William Still and other UGRR workers then sent the couple on to Boston, where Ellen and William lived for nearly two years. After the Fugitive Slave Law of 1850 was enacted, slave catchers tried to capture the Crafts in Boston. The UGRR helped the Crafts sail to England, where they lived for nineteen years. Not until 1869, after all the slaves had been freed, did the Crafts return to the United States.

office in Philadelphia. Still and three other men opened the lid, and out popped Brown. Because of the way he escaped, Henry became known as Box Brown.

There were many other "sad and thrilling stories," as Still said, about UGRR escapes. Thousands of American homes still have secret rooms where runaway slaves once hid. Thousands of families have **ancestors** who worked on the UGRR or escaped with its help.

Despite the label, "This side up with care," Henry "Box" Brown actually rode the train for a time while upside down.

The South Strikes Back

Slave owners struck back at UGRR workers. After helping Box Brown escape, Samuel A. Smith tried to ship more slaves to the North in crates. Smith was caught and sent to the Richmond jail. He remained imprisoned for seven years.

William Still's friend Samuel D. Burris was an UGRR conductor. Like Still, Burris was a free black man. He often went to Delaware, where slavery was legal, and led slaves north to freedom. Burris was caught and jailed in Dover, Delaware, for more than a year. As his punishment for rescuing slaves, he was sentenced to be sold into slavery himself. Luckily, an abolitionist bought him for five hundred dollars and set him free.

Some UGRR workers met violent deaths. A conductor named Seth Concklin went down to Alabama to bring relatives of Still's to freedom. Concklin led the four slaves to Indiana, where they were captured. Concklin and the slaves were sent back to Alabama by boat. On the way, Concklin drowned in the Ohio River. It appears one of his guards pushed him off the boat.

Meanwhile, in the mid-1800s, arguments over slavery grew more heated. Southern slave owners claimed that the 1793 Fugitive Slave Law was too weak. They wanted a stronger law to help them capture more runaways. **Pro-slavery** people also wanted new states in the nation to allow slavery. Abolitionists wanted slavery banned in new states.

In 1850 the U.S. Congress passed a series of acts called the **Compromise** of 1850. Lawmakers passed these acts to keep the peace between the North and the South. First, California was admitted to the union as a free state. This pleased abolitionists in the North. On September 18, President Millard Fillmore signed a new law that pleased Southern slave owners. The Fugitive Slave Law of 1850 required federal marshals and other officials to help slave hunters. Anyone who hid or helped a fugitive slave could be jailed for six months and fined two thousand dollars.

Runaways on U.S. soil were now in great danger of being **seized** and returned to slavery. The new law did not scare off UGRR workers,

Slave hunters had government support in their quest to capture escaped slaves.

however. In fact, they were busier than ever. They helped large numbers of runaway slaves flee to Canada. Slavery had been outlawed there in 1834.

Some slaves felt that not even Canada was safe. A number of African Americans, including Box Brown, put themselves out of reach of capture by sailing three thousand miles to England.

Abraham Lincoln is shown standing with a group of former slaves outside the White House.

Slaveholders were enraged that the UGRR kept helping slaves escape. The 100,000 slaves who fled between the early 1800s and 1860 were worth a total of about $50 million. What right did abolitionists have to **deprive** the South of such valuable property? Abolitionists were just as enraged. How could the U.S. government continue to tolerate slavery?

Finally, in 1861, the arguing over slavery and other issues sparked a war. The Civil War, or the War Between the States, was fought between the North and the South. In 1865 the North triumphed under President Abraham Lincoln. This victory ended slavery in the United States. The mission of the Underground Railroad was complete.

Glossary

abolitionist—A person who is determined to end slavery.

ancestors—A person's relatives from a long time ago.

antislavery—Against slavery.

bondage—The state of being a slave or prisoner.

compromise—A solution to a disagreement where each side gets some of what it wants and gives up some of what it wants.

declaration—An announcement or statement.

deprive—To take something away from someone.

federal—Relating to the central government of a nation.

fugitive—Someone who has escaped.

illegal—Against the law.

liberty—Freedom.

plantations—Large farms.

population—The number of people in a place.

pro-slavery—Wanting slavery to be a legal practice.

protested—Spoke or acted against.

resolution—A formal statement put forth by a group.

seized—Grabbed or captured.

slavery—The practice of owning people.

Timeline

1607—England settles Virginia, its first American colony

1619—Slavery begins in Virginia

1688—People in Germantown, Pennsylvania, pass the first resolution condemning slavery in the present-day United States

1733—Britain establishes Georgia, its thirteenth and final American colony

1770s—The colonial slave population reaches half a million

1776—The Declaration of Independence announces the birth of the United States but does nothing to end slavery

1780—Massachusetts becomes the first state to outlaw slavery

1787—Lawmakers create the U.S. Constitution, which largely ignores the slavery issue

1793—The Fugitive Slave Law makes it a federal crime to help a slave escape

1800—The United States has 900,000 slaves, mostly in the South

1619   *1776*   *1793*

Early 1800s—A network of people and hiding places begins helping large numbers of slaves escape

1830s—The slave-escape network becomes known as the Underground Railroad

1850—The second Fugitive Slave Law makes it easier for owners to capture runaway slaves anywhere on U.S. soil; the Underground Railroad begins to send many fugitive slaves to Canada

1861—The North and South begin the Civil War as a result of arguing over issues involving slavery

1865—**April 9:** The Union wins the Civil War
December 6: The Thirteenth Amendment goes into effect, and all slaves are free

1913—Famed Underground Railroad conductor Harriet Tubman dies in Auburn, New York, at about age ninety-one.

2015—Americans celebrate the 150th anniversary of the end of the Civil War and the freeing of the last American slaves

1830s   *1865*   *2015*

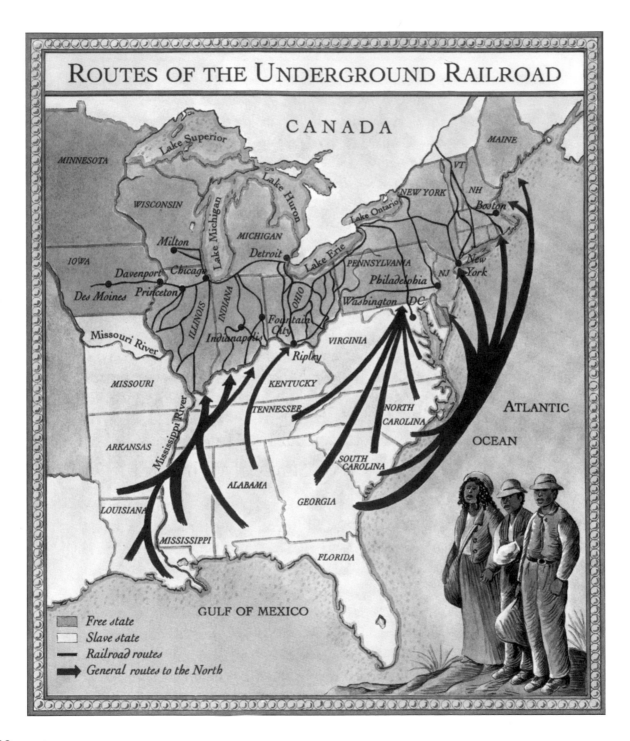

ROUTES OF THE UNDERGROUND RAILROAD

CANADA

MINNESOTA

Lake Superior

WISCONSIN

IOWA

Milton

Davenport

Des Moines

Princeton

Chicago

Lake Michigan

MICHIGAN

Detroit

Lake Huron

Lake Erie

MAINE

VT

NEW YORK

NH

Boston

Lake Ontario

PENNSYLVANIA

NJ

New York

Philadelphia

Washington

DC

ILLINOIS

INDIANA

OHIO

Indianapolis

Fountain City

Missouri River

Ripley

VIRGINIA

MISSOURI

KENTUCKY

ATLANTIC

Mississippi River

TENNESSEE

NORTH CAROLINA

OCEAN

ARKANSAS

SOUTH CAROLINA

LOUISIANA

ALABAMA

GEORGIA

MISSISSIPPI

FLORIDA

GULF OF MEXICO

Free state
Slave state
Railroad routes
General routes to the North

42

Further Information

B O O K S

Fradin, Dennis Brindell. *Bound for the North Star: True Stories of Fugitive Slaves*. New York: Clarion Books, 2000.

Fradin, Judith Bloom, and Dennis Brindell Fradin. *5,000 Miles to Freedom: Ellen and William Craft's Flight from Slavery*. Washington, DC: National Geographic, 2006.

Klingel, Cynthia. *Harriet Tubman: Abolitionist and Underground Railroad Conductor*. Chanhassen, MN: Child's World, 2004.

Landau, Elaine. *Fleeing to Freedom on the Underground Railroad: The Courageous Slaves, Agents, and Conductors*. Minneapolis: Twenty-First Century Books, 2006.

Rossi, Ann. *Freedom Struggle: The Anti-Slavery Movement in America, 1830–1865*. Washington, DC: National Geographic, 2005.

WEB SITES

A PBS site with a wealth of information on slavery and the Underground Railroad:
http://www.pbs.org/wgbh/aia/part4/4p2944.html

The National Park Service's "Aboard the Underground Railroad" site that describes the Underground Railroad and historic places connected with it:
http://www.cr.nps.gov/nr/travel/underground/

This National Geographic site about the Underground Railroad re-creates what it was like to be a fugitive slave:
http://www.nationalgeographic.com/railroad/

For a biography of Harriet Tubman:
http://www.nyhistory.com/harriettubman/life.htm

Information about Levi and Catherine Coffin and their Underground Railroad station in Indiana:
http://www.waynet.org/nonprofit/coffin.htm

Bibliography

Bentley, Judith. *"Dear Friend": Thomas Garrett and William Still, Collaborators on the Underground Railroad*. New York: Cobblehill, 1997.

Bradford, Sarah. *Harriet Tubman: The Moses of Her People*. Secaucus, NJ: Citadel Press, 1974.

Brandt, Nat. *The Town That Started the Civil War*. New York: Laurel, 1991.

Brown, Henry. *Narrative of Henry Box Brown*. Philadelphia: Rhistoric Publications, 1969.

Coffin, Levi. *Reminiscences of Levi Coffin*. Richmond, IN: Friends United Press, 1991.

Craft, William, and Ellen Craft. *Running a Thousand Miles for Freedom*. New York: Arno Press and the New York Times, 1969.

Jefferson, Paul, ed. *The Travels of William Wells Brown*. Edinburgh, Scotland: Edinburgh University Press, 1991.

Larson, Kate Clifford. *Bound for the Promised Land: Harriet Tubman, Portrait of an American Hero*. New York: Ballantine Books, 2004.

Pickard, Kate. *The Kidnapped and the Ransomed*. Philadelphia: The Jewish Publication Society of America, 1970.

Sterling, Dorothy. *Black Foremothers: Three Lives*. New York: Feminist Press, 1988.

Still, William. *The Underground Railroad*. New York: Arno Press and the New York Times, 1968.

Two Biographies by African-American Women (includes reprint of 1856 edition of *Biography of an American Bondman* by Josephine Brown). New York: Oxford University Press, 1991.

Index

Page numbers in **boldface** are illustrations.

maps
    Origin of African Slaves, **8**
    Routes of the Underground
      Railroad, **42**
    Slave and Free States, **24**

abolitionists, 7, 20, 21, 25, 33, 34,
    37
abolition of slavery, 16, 20, 34
American colonies, slavery in, 7, 9
American Indians, 9

Brown, Henry "Box", 30–31, **32,** 35
Burris, Samuel D., 33
buying freedom, 13

Canada, 23, 35
children, 11, 29
Civil War, the, 37
code, speaking in, 25
Coffin, Catherine and Levi, 27–28,
    28
Compromise of 1850, 34
Concklin, Seth, 34
Constitution, U.S., 16
Craft, Ellen and William, 31

Declaration of Independence, **14,**
    15

England, 7, 31, 35

families, slave, 11, 13
field hands, **10,** 11
Fillmore, Millard, 34
free blacks, 13, 33
free states, 16, 21–23, **24,** 25, 34
Fugitive Slave Laws (1793 and
    1850), 16–17, 31, 34–35

Garrett, Thomas, 29

hiding places, 22, **23,** 27–28, 31
house slaves, 11–12, **12**

laws, slaves and, 12–13, 16–17, 31,
    34–35
Lincoln, Abraham, **36,** 37

Mexico, 20

names, of slaves, 12–13, 23
North Star, the, 20, 28

owners, of slaves, 11, 12–13, 16–17,
    33

Pennsylvania Anti-Slavery Society,
    30, 31
population, of slaves, 9, 16
property, slaves as, 11, 12–13, 37
punishments, 11, 13, 33–34

religion, 20
rewards, 16, 29
rights, of slaves, 12–13
runaway slaves, 13, 16, 17, 19, 21, 26
    Fugitive Slave Laws and, 16–17,
      34–35
    Underground Railroad and,
      20–23, 25, 27–31

secret rooms, 22, **23,** 27–28, 31
signals, 21
slave hunters, 16, 22–23, **26,** 27–28,
    31, 34, **35**
slavery, 7, 9, **10,** 11–13
    See also runaway slaves
slave states, 16, 20, **24,** 34
slave trade, **6**
Smith, Samuel A., 30, 33
states, new, 34
stationmasters, 25, 27–28
stations, **18,** 21, **22, 23,** 25
Still, William, **30,** 31

Tubman, Harriet, 28–29, **29**

Underground Railroad, 19–25,
    27–31

About the Author

Dennis Fradin is the author of 150 books, some of them written with his wife, Judith Bloom Fradin. Their book for Clarion, *The Power of One: Daisy Bates and the Little Rock Nine*, was named a Golden Kite Honor Book. Another of Dennis's well-known books is *Let It Begin Here! Lexington & Concord: First Battles of the American Revolution*, published by Walker. Other recent books by the Fradins include *Jane Addams: Champion of Democracy* for Clarion and *5,000 Miles to Freedom: Ellen and William Craft's Flight from Slavery* for National Geographic Children's Books. Their current project for National Geographic is the *Witness to Disaster* series about natural disasters. *Turning Points in U.S. History* is Dennis's first series for Marshall Cavendish Benchmark. The Fradins have three grown children and five grandchildren.